Be
Jamison

SCANDAL–PSALM 51

CREATE

RENEW

RESTORE

After the Rain
Publishing LLC

J.T. WALLINGTON

Visit me at jtwallington.com.

For more titles from After the Rain Publishing LLC, visit:
aftertherainpublishing.com.

SCANDAL –PSALM 51

DAY 1

MOTIVE

It happened in the spring of the year, at the time when kings go out to battle, that David ... remained at Jerusalem.
–2 Samuel 11:1

D id you ever plan to do something but changed your mind and did something else? In this introductory page to this devotional, we find David's motive for writing Psalm 51. As king, he was supposed to go to war but stayed home instead. This simple choice removed him from the physical battlefield but forced him into a far more destructive battle with his mind—a battle that affected everyone he loved and lasted the rest of his life.

The story is found in 2 Samuel 11 and 12. Good King David's scandal began when he seduced a married woman into sleeping with him. When she began to show, he desperately tried to cover up his affair by ensuring that her husband, who was also his best soldier, was killed in battle. I encourage you to read this story prior to continuing with this devotional.

Throughout the coming days, we will find that even through the driving rain of guilt for our personal sins, there is hope. If we turn our cry of despair into a cry for God's forgiveness, we will eventually find that our tears were seeds that slowly, almost imperceptibly, bloom into brilliant flowers of renewal.

DAY 2

BROKEN

He tried to put it back together the best he could. He tried everything—glue, duct tape—but it just wouldn't be fixed. The vase that had held countless flowers from past generations, the vase that had been passed from great-grandmas to grandmas to moms to daughters—lay shattered on the floor.

What really can be done with it? The broken vase is a visible example of the preciousness and fragility of the life we live. Sometimes our choices bring serious consequences and shatter the vase. We are unable to put the pieces back together—and even if we could, the scars of that shattered existence remain.

This devotional explores our brokenness in the context of Psalm 51. In this psalm, King David confessed and searched for repentance after committing not only adultery but also premeditated murder. After the death of his firstborn, David penned his opening line:

Have mercy upon me, O God.
—Psalm 51:1

DAY 3

DROWNING IN MERCY

E ver been to one of the two oceans that bookend the United States? Then you've seen the waves crash upon the sandy shore. Wave after wave rolls in and breaks, startling the sand and covering the trail of footprints behind you.

David cried out to God after his sins, his breaking of God's law, and the resulting guilt he felt: "Have mercy upon me, O God" (Psalm 51:1).

He was asking God to act, begging Him to complete the first step in the recovery of his soul, an act only God can do. David was pleading with God to pour out His mercy like the waves of the ocean upon his sinful ways that left him broken and lost.

Watching the waves crashing on the shoreline, we realize we have absolutely no control over those waves. To receive mercy, we must first recognize that we cannot scoop ourselves out of our despair or desperate moments.

Like the waves, God's mercy crashes over us with its allotted force. When you've cried out to God, begging for His mercy, you've done all you can do. Now feel the wave of mercy soak you:

According to Your lovingkindness.
—Psalm 51:1

HE LOVES

I am not a big fan of receiving gifts. I love to give them, but when it's my turn to open the package at the Christmas tree, my heart always sinks. Maybe I feel nervous about not liking what someone got me, or maybe I feel I'm not good enough for someone to spend hard-earned cash on me.

"According to Your lovingkindness" (Psalm 51:1). Lovingkindness comes from the Hebrew word *hesed.* The Bible first uses this word in Genesis 19, when God's lovingkindness saved Lot from the destruction of his hometown of Sodom by sending angels to direct him to leave.

God's lovingkindness is a gift He is eager to pour out on us, but *hesed* is more than a gift.

From the very beginning, God proposed an agreement with His people: He would be their God and they would be His people. Just as Lot had to leave Sodom to receive *hesed*, we must also make a commitment. Hesed represents a contractual relationship between God and His people.

In this relationship, when we stumble and fall, He loves:

> *According to the multitude of Your tender mercies.*
> *–Psalm 51:1*

MORE THAN ENOUGH

W e've already talked about the waves of mercy God wants to pour into our lives, but we feel those waves drench us with David's next words here in Psalm 51. Not only does God respond actively with powerful mercy when we ask for His forgiveness, but that mercy is in abundance: in "the multitude of [His] tender mercies" (Psalm 51:1).

If you have driven a car, you know this simple truth: You will run out of gas (or charge) at some point and will have to fill up (or charge up). It doesn't matter how good of a driver you are, how few speeding tickets you've received, or even if you've never had an accident.

Just like gas in the car, we need God's mercy. But unlike gas, it doesn't run out! God gives mercy more plentifully than Niagara Falls gives water. He gives mercy as if it were the very air we need to breathe, and it exists in greater supply than we could ever use up.

David wanted his readers to know that regardless of their sins, God's mercy is the only medicine that can heal those sins, and that it doesn't run out. We need the multitude of His tender mercies to:

> *Blot out my transgressions.*
> *–Psalm 51:1*

DAY 6

WIPED CLEAN

I 've got to have a clean windshield. Let's just say the blue windshield washer fluid under my hood never lasts from one oil change to the next. With all the driving I do, it's not long before my windshield is speckled with bugs, dust, and debris. Then I spray that blue fluid and watch eagerly as all those pesky inhibitors of clear vision get wiped away.

"Blot out my transgressions" (Psalm 51:1). The Hebrew word for blot in this sense means to wipe away and make clean—like the wipers on my windshield. Having established that God abounds in mercy and covenantal love, David cried out to that same God in eager petition for his transgressions to be wiped away.

But what exactly is a transgression? Here the Hebrew word means wantonness, or not giving heed to what is right. In other words, David knew that adultery, which ultimately led to premeditated murder, was wrong, but he didn't care and performed his deed anyway. Now David begged God to wipe away his wantonness and to:

Wash me thoroughly from my iniquity.
—Psalm 51:2

LAUNDRY DAY

D avid knew there is more to being forgiven than making a onetime plea for a sin to be blotted out. He knew he must also ask God, "Wash me thoroughly from my iniquity" (Psalm 51:2).

The Hebrew word for wash tells us that David was giving God permission to wash him from his iniquity. "Washed" also means putting on new clothes. David was giving God permission to remove his old clothes of self-indulgent sin and to replace them with clean ones.

We saw yesterday that David asked God to blot out his transgression, but then he asked to be cleansed from his "iniquity"—an entirely different word.

Iniquity is the guilt caused by sin. David was guilty, feeling the burden of his transgression of wantonness, and now that guilt was sitting on his shoulders like a boulder, threatening to crush him.

So he cried out to God: Strip me of these old clothes encrusted with the putrid stench of guilt and replace them with clean, fresh clothes straight from the dryer so that I can breathe in the refreshing scent of freedom. In other words:

Cleanse me from my sin.
–Psalm 51:2

SPRING CLEANING

S o far, we have seen that David wanted his sin blotted out, recognizing that his debt must be paid. He also realized that his sin had caused him guilt that only God can remove; only God could change his dirty clothes.

Then David moved even further into seeking forgiveness by asking God to cleanse him. David had already listed three characteristics of God in the opening of this psalm (mercy, lovingkindness, and tender mercies). He then presented a second trilogy of words (blot, wash, and cleanse). "Cleanse" carries the concept of making pure or free from sin. David's guilt moved him to plead, "Cleanse me from my sin" (Psalm 51:2).

When you clean your house, you understand one thing: it takes time. It takes time to scrub the toilet, to fold the laundry, to vacuum. It is hard, sweaty, tiring work. David asked God to cleanse him, knowing it would be a process, and he allowed God the time to cleanse him. Every dust bunny of sin must be removed, every lust of the heart polished clean, every moment of defeat from succumbing to his transgression must be picked up and thrown out. It took time, but David said:

> *I acknowledge my transgressions.*
> *—Psalm 51:3*

BE BOLD BEFORE GOD

David betrayed his best soldier by having an affair with his wife and then ordering his murder to cover it up. When you have done something as horrible as David did, it can seem that life is unbearable and that you have no right to forgiveness. But you must remember one thing: no sin is greater than another. An affair is weighed the same as gossip and lying and using God's name in vain.

David's experience teaches us an important lesson about God's forgiveness. He had a right to go to God's throne and receive forgiveness because he was willing to acknowledge his transgressions. Jesus would say that it is the sick who need a physician, not the healthy. (See Matthew 9:12.) Acknowledging our wrong gives us the right to go boldly before God's throne for His forgiveness.

We must remove the chip of arrogance from our shoulder and be willing to admit our faults. If I point at someone else when it was I who broke the vase, I am not acknowledging my transgression and am inhibiting God from forgiving me. With David I must admit:

My sin is always before me.
–Psalm 51:3

SPEED LIMIT

I knew it was wrong. I saw the speed limit signs, but I did it anyway—I drove 78 miles per hour in a 65-mile-per-hour zone and got a $200 fine. I ignored the law and paid the price. I knew the consequences of my actions, but I didn't slow down. Every day after that, I warily eyed the mailman because I knew that ticket was coming. It was all I could think about. With David, I groaned, "My sin is always before me" (Psalm 51:3).

Some believe it took David six months to a year to compose this psalm of repentance, which would have given him plenty of time to think about what he had done. We have seen that "transgression" means not giving heed to what is right, and that "iniquity" is the resulting guilt. He had broken God's law, and I imagine all he could think about was that proverbial speeding ticket coming in the mail.

While his sin certainly involved others, David knew, every moment of every day and night, that ultimately, his sin was against the Lawgiver.

> *Against You, You only, have I sinned.*
> *—Psalm 51:4*

AGAINST YOU

That summer sun beat down on my bare back. I knew it was not the brightest idea to work in the garden without a shirt under the noonday Southern California sun, but I did it anyway. My then-wife, with every inch of skin protected, worked diligently alongside me. Although I could feel my skin beginning to smolder, I convinced myself that since I would be out there just a few more minutes, I would be fine.

"Against You, You only, have I sinned" (Psalm 51:4). The sun targeted the ground, the garden vegetables, my wife, and me with the very same intensity. Yet a week later, I was the only one peeling dead skin off my broiled back.

David's sin affected Bathsheba. She lost her honor, her husband, and later her baby. David's sin also affected Uriah, Bathsheba's husband. He lost his beautiful wife, the prospect of raising a family, and even his life.

Although that sun beat down on all things around me, it affected me most deeply. Our sins affect those around us, but God is affected most deeply, as He bore them in His Son. With David we cry:

Against You, You only, have I sinned, and done this evil in Your sight.
–Psalm 51:4

DAY 12

A LAW OF LOVE

As his affair and act of murder screamed in his mind, David penned these words: "Against You, You only, have I sinned, and done this evil in Your sight" (Psalm 51:4).

So many times we think our actions are our responsibility alone. But this is a lie. A moral, selfless code exists for us to protect others, not hurt them. And although following this code naturally blesses us, our motivation for following it should be the benefit of others.

David tried to cover up his affair and subsequent impregnating of a married man's wife. And much to his distress, Uriah was more loyal to the great King David than David had been to those he was called to serve as king.

God had spelled out His desire for His children in the Decalogue, a law that David had shattered. Yet as the natural consequences of breaking this moral code of blessing wrapped their bitter arms around him, we see the first buds of a deep love for God's law in his insistence for God to uphold it:

> *That You may be found just when You speak,*
> *and blameless when You judge.*
> *—Psalm 51:4*

MY FAULT

ead hung low, face stained with tears, and conscience capsized in an ocean of guilt, David acknowledged that he could blame only himself for his actions.

David knew that God's law was not to blame for his remorse. It was clear to him that pointing fingers at God, as Adam and Eve had done in Eden (Genesis 3), would be to no avail; blaming an innocent God for humankind's actions is simply foolishness.

The universe was watching. But if that's too dramatic, certainly all of God's people were watching to see what the good King David would do next. Would the beloved monarch sell out God's law and claim that it wasn't fair to be placed under such restrictions? After all, the king's word was next to God's in the ancient culture.

Instead, David gulped down any pride his status gave him. He acknowledged that he blew it, that his human passions clouded his judgment and led him to commit sins that would echo down the halls of history.

> *Behold, I was brought forth in iniquity,*
> *and in sin my mother conceived me.*
> *–Psalm 51:5*

ALWAYS A SINNER

David didn't blame his egregious sins on a momentary lapse of judgment. Rather, he approached the Almighty with a heavy heart, admitting he had been a sinner long before: "Behold, I was brought forth in iniquity, and in sin my mother conceived me" (Psalm 51:5).

Temptation to sin is often followed by an equally strong temptation to say: "God, Your law is too hard; it cannot be followed." Even when we follow it to the best of our ability, we still stumble. So what hope do we have to keep God's law?

We need to stop primping in front of the mirror, combing or curling our own image of perfection. The solid truth is, regardless how hard we try, we will fail. And the longer we stand in front of the mirror, the longer we will see only our disappointments. We need to look higher—to Christ and His victory on the Cross.

Only when we admit our struggles, our failings, that we are not perfect, can God start to rebuild us. Then David's words will be ours:

> *You desire truth in the inward parts, and in the hidden part*
> *You will make me to know wisdom.*
> *—Psalm 51:6*

HIDDEN TRUTH

We need to stop fooling ourselves. If teaching has taught me anything, it is that we all struggle with something. All of my students come from a difficult background and it takes a long time for them to admit to me their issues. How many of us wear a mask in public pretending everything is A-OK when in fact it is not?

David's words to God still apply to us today: "You desire truth in the inward parts, and in the hidden part You will make me to know wisdom" (Psalm 51:6). We need to be honest with ourselves and with others. Francesca Battistelli has a new song at the time of this writing entitled, If We're Honest. The premise: we need to stop lying to each other.

David admitted that his royal robes could not hide his human flesh. He confessed that he had always been a sinner, and we need to do the same. And when we cast off whatever "royal robe" we hide behind, God will make us to "know wisdom."

In David's admission of guilt, he was admitting that he had a problem—his humanity—for way too long. Now that David came clean, God could make him clean. He asked God:

> *Purge me with hyssop, and I shall be clean.*
> *–Psalm 51:7*

DAY 16

MULLIGAN

R eal golf? I have never played it. I have played miniature golf, and I have played golf video games, but I have never been on the green with the breeze blowing and having to address the ball for the perfect swing. However, in these virtual golf environments, I have heard the term "mulligan."

Being the avid researcher I am, Wikipedia tells me that "a mulligan is a second chance to perform an action, usually after the first chance went wrong through bad luck or a blunder." That same online search will bring up the Professional Golf Association's confirming definition: "any 'do-over,' or second chance after initial failure."

"Purge me with hyssop, and I shall be clean" (Psalm 51:7). David prayed for a second chance, a do-over, a mulligan. To be purged with hyssop means "to de-sin" or "un-sin"—to become pure by God cleaning out the inward parts of our humanity.

Don't we all have something in our closets that makes us need a do-over? If only I could change the past—my regret haunts me. Well, Jesus offers the hyssop, the de-sinning, the mulligan we all so desperately need. We just need to ask Him to:

> *Wash me, and I shall be whiter than snow.*
> *—Psalm 51:7*

SNOWING

Fall is a pretty time of year—until the constant rain turns everything to mush, transforming the scenery into just mud. But it doesn't last long, since the next season is winter, and in over half of the United States, snow covers the mud. Snow falls gently (except for the occasional blizzard) and covers everything it touches.

Snow also accumulates; it piles up. You fall asleep with dead grass and bare trees outside your window and wake up to a white winter wonderland. "Wash me, and I shall be whiter than snow" (Psalm 51:7).

As we saw in verse 1, David begged to be cleansed. But this time, he recognized that the cleansing leaves no patch of mud uncovered, no dead blade of grass visible, no branch naked. His shame was covered. Just as snow covers the multitude of surfaces, so God cleanses us by covering our sins with the blood of Jesus.

It is only when we allow God to cleanse us and cover our sins that we, as guilty sinners, can look to heaven and ask God to:

Make me hear joy and gladness.
—Psalm 51:8

JOY AND GLADNESS

Make me hear joy and gladness" (Psalm 51:8). Joy and gladness are the result of an action, and it wasn't an action David could do. In the previous verse, we saw David wanting his muddy self to be washed and made whiter than snow. Joy and gladness come from freedom from sin in one's life, and they don't occur by the sinner's wish but by God's forgiving action.

But there was more to David's plea. He didn't want only joy and gladness—he wanted to hear them, to experience them.

The story is told of a man who committed a horrible sin. Unable to forgive himself, he could not hear the joy and gladness in heaven over his prospective repentance (Luke 15:7).

But David had already repented. He was remorseful and wanted God's help in hearing the joy and gladness from the streets of heaven over his decision to simply say, "I'm here God—save me."

David's sins taught him that joy and gladness come from broken bones.

That the bones You have broken may rejoice.
—Psalm 51:8

BROKEN BONES

I t hurts—I can still feel the pain.

At age ten, I was roller-skating in the school gymnasium when my friend dared me to grab onto the climbing rope as I skated by for a boost of speed. I let go of the rope too late, landed on my wrist, and broke the bones that connect my hand to my arm. My wrist was paralyzed. My mind told my hand to move but it simply wouldn't.

Broken bones hurt. David's prayer was "that the bones You have broken may rejoice" (Psalm 51:8).

Rejoicing over broken bones seems impossible to me. But this is exactly what David did. He understood that even in pain, re-joicing can come. He was rejoicing, not because of the pain, but because God was forming something better inside him. David understood that even in his sins of adultery and murder, God had not left him.

The breaking of bones promises hope. My doctor had to painfully pull the bones in my paralyzed wrist back into alignment so they would heal correctly. David's heart was paralyzed by his inten-tional sins. God had to pull his heart back into alignment so that he could experience the joy of healing.

Next, David pleaded for God to:

> *Hide Your face from my sins.*
> *–Psalm 51:9*

DON'T REMIND ME

David would never forget. How could he?

We saw in verse 3 a few days ago that David's sin was always before him. What a hideous memory would sit and rot in his mind! But David prayed to God: "Hide Your face from my sins" (Psalm 51:9).

Hiding the face is a metaphor for turning away. David didn't ask God to turn away from him but from his sins. God hides His face from our sins, not from us. David was seeking utter forgiveness, the type of forgiveness in which sins are tossed into the depths of the sea or removed as far as the east is from the west. (See Micah 7:19 and Psalm 103:12).

The beauty of God turning away from your sins is that He simply doesn't see them anymore. If you have ever tried to take a picture facing the sun, you know what it is like to turn away from it. The brightness no longer blinding you, the intensity of the light now behind you, you are freed from the overwhelming effects of the sun. When God hides His face by turning away from your sins, He is relieved. He has your permission to forgive you, to:

> *Blot out all my iniquities.*
> *—Psalm 51:9*

LET'S PAINT

Painting is a time of great excitement for my two toddlers—and of great messes for me. My kids love to get paint everywhere. Magically, the beige carpet becomes a rainbow, the marble counter a blue ocean, and the tan walls green bushes. It is obvious when toddlers paint; the paint gets everywhere—and boy does it stand out against the muted earth tones of the rest of the house!

Today's verse is a repeat from the psalmist. He again pleaded for his heavenly Father to "blot out all my iniquities" (Psalm 51:9).

David's sins were noticeable to God, and of course, to himself. David desperately wanted these splotches removed—scrubbed off the walls. He begged God to not only turn and hide His face from them, but also remove them as if they had never occurred. How many times I have had to endure cleaning up the paint of two toddlers. How much more has God had to clean up, blot out, and wipe away, the sins of my own life. But each time He cleans up my messes, I start to learn from my mistakes and am slowly becoming the masterpiece He designed me to be. Mess by mess, God is answering my prayer to:

Create in me a clean heart.
—Psalm 51:10

TIME TO CREATE

Turmoil. Chaos. Emptiness. Loneliness. While these emotions describe how David felt, they also point to the Bible's description of Earth prior to Creation. David knew that God alone can create, so he asked Him to take these emotions and create a new heart, a clean heart, within him.

So often we try to create our own forgiveness. We believe that if we pray hard enough, bargaining with God long enough, that we can earn it. We will forgive ourselves only after we self-torture with grief, regret, or even depression. But David relinquished control. David asked for a creation—a creation of his very heart. To give up control is not easy; it is uncomfortable. We want control, we want a say in what the new heart will look like. We want to be the contractor of ourselves. In futile attempts, we try to build our own sanctification.

To get a clean heart, we must put down the hammer and simply ask and allow God to create—not re-create or remodel or reform—a clean heart inside. And then, once our new heart is in place, with David we can ask God to:

Renew a steadfast spirit within me.
−Psalm 51:10

DAY 23

TIME TO REPLACE

E very couple of months my refrigerator reminds me that it is time to replace the water filter.

A light comes on that says "replace" and off to the hardware store I go. If it weren't for that light, I would likely leave that filter in place for longer than the manufacturer's recommendation. After all, the water doesn't taste any different, and it doesn't pour any different. It doesn't seem to affect me in any way besides that little red light on the door. But if you are like me and have tried to save money on filters, you know that over time the water does taste different, it pours at a slower rate, and that red light never stops blinking.

"Renew a steadfast spirit within me" (Psalm 51:10). David's spirit was crushed—clogged by his actions. The "red light" was blinking and he asked God to replace his spirit. Sometimes we would live in our guilt or depression forever, never asking for a change. And slowly, almost imperceptibly, we lose our ability to taste joy. The only way we know what's happening is by that blinking light. And when we let God replace our spirit, we can then say:

> *Do not cast me away from Your presence.*
> *–Psalm 51:10*

REMEMBER ME

I n her later years, my grandmother developed Alzheimer's Disease and began losing her short-term memory. Instead of seeing me as her grandson, she thought I was her son (my father). As the years passed, the disease ravaged more and more of her mind until she didn't remember most of us at all.

"Do not cast me away from Your presence" (Psalm 51:11). The Hebrew word for cast carries the idea of being thrown out, disposed of, and even expelled. Pretty harsh. Just as my grandmother in her diseased state threw memories of me away and therefore lost a relationship with me, David was fearful that God would throw him away and remember him no more.

Ultimately, David desired an intimate relationship with God. In one of David's darkest and most depressed times, he still sought God's presence. After asking for a re-created heart and new spirit, or attitude, so he could begin again and refocus himself, David asked God to stay by his side. David was seeking a Ruler to govern his life and therefore asked:

> *Do not take Your Holy Spirit from me.*
> *—Psalm 51:11*

RULE OVER ME

Given the choice of driving or being a passenger, I'll choose driving every time. I love the feel of the steering wheel in my grip, the touch of the pedal under my foot, and my car accelerating or slowing at my command. The ability to move my car in any direction I desire is one of the joys of my life.

"Do not take Your Holy Spirit from me" (Psalm 51:11). David had been in control of his own life. He chose to sleep with a married woman and to have her husband killed because of his desire for control. Much like I would always pick driving over being the passenger, David picked his desire over God's desire. Now David realized that he must have someone else rule his life, for he was incapable of ruling by his own will and having it turn out right.

How often we need to pray this prayer—that God not take away His Holy Spirit! If only David had whispered it when he saw the beautiful Bathsheba taking a bath. If only I would whisper it when temptation comes my way. David now prayed that in his future interactions, God would be in control of his decisions through His Spirit. David knew that only under God's control could his request be fulfilled:

Restore to me the joy of Your salvation.
–Psalm 51:12

DAY 26

IT'S "V-DAY"

We love to mark holidays. We have Christmas every December and the Fourth of July circled on our calendars each year. We enjoy the celebrations of New Year's Day and we embrace the holidays of Labor Day and Memorial Day as days free from work—although their meanings go much deeper than shopping and barbeques.

One day we seem to neglect in our—dare I say it—millennial generation, is V-day: Victory Day, a holiday to celebrate the end of World War II.

In our psalm, David asked God to grant him a holiday. "Restore to me the joy of Your salvation" (Psalm 51:12). At first glance, there's nothing about a holiday here, just another plea for forgiveness. But David's plea goes much, much deeper. The word salvation comes from a Hebrew word that includes the meaning of "accepting help" as well as "being victorious." David was praying for a V-day!

David prayed that God would give him back the joy of a victorious life. Like David, we must recognize that victory in life does not come by our own hands, but by God's. The psalm shows David's continued need for God's hand:

Uphold me by Your generous Spirit.
—Psalm 51:12

REMODELING

A s a child, my family owned a five-bedroom farmhouse in Northern Minnesota that we rented out. The tenants didn't take very good care of it, so our family spent a Christmas vacation remodeling the whole thing.

"Uphold me by Your generous Spirit" (Psalm 51:12). We have seen repeatedly in this psalm that David could not cure himself, forgive himself, nor make it by himself—he needed God.

David was weak. David was tired. David had been depressed for a long time because of his actions. He continued to call out to God in this psalm, but his focus began shifting from the past to the future. David knew he would need God to "uphold" him because he could not stand in his run-down condition. Just as the tenant damage caused the old farmhouse to need remodeling, we damage our lives and need someone to come in and remodel the whole thing.

David sought this out from God; he wanted God to come into his life and rebuild him, to strengthen him, to hold him up. He asked God to remake him by His Spirit so that he no longer acted according to his own desires. Only then could David:

> *Teach transgressors Your ways.*
> *—Psalm 51:13*

TEACHER

I made a mistake—a very, very big mistake.

Alongside David, I moaned, groaned, and wanted God to do something to help me recover from my big mistake. Just like you, I am a sinner. This isn't surprising, but I don't think we recognize just how sinful we really are. Beyond that, I don't think we acknowledge our sinfulness. We are not open enough with others about our mistakes. We have seen that David begged for forgiveness and newness of life. Now he wanted to "teach transgressors Your ways" (Psalm 51:13).

This was something different—something deeper—than simply giving an offering for forgiveness. David knew that his life must be the offering to God, which would give him the opportunity to be a lesson for others. He asked God to renew his heart and create a new attitude inside him so that others could recognize their need of redemption.

My mistake needs to be your lesson and yours mine. We need each other, in community, to be honest and open, so that we can learn from each other. The combined lessons of our mistakes can encourage others to avoid them. When we are honest with others about our history:

Sinners shall be converted to You.
—Psalm 51:13

CONVERTED

Converted. Some see this word as a roadblock to salvation. To others it means they must totally change to be acceptable to God. And others think it is the unachievable result of spotless obedience to God's law. David asked that God use his affair and murder so that "sinners shall be converted to You" (Psalm 51:13).

The word in Hebrew simply means to return. David didn't want wayward sinners to wander farther and farther from God's eternal love. He wanted to use his life lessons to show that no matter what they have done, they can come back to God.

You have not wandered so far that you cannot return to God. Good King David committed adultery and murder. Abraham, the father of God's Old Testament people, told lies and slept with his wife's nurse. Moses, who talked with God face to face, killed someone with his own hands. And each of them returned to God. These and other Bible heroes learned to be converted daily. They knew they would wander into sin again and again—and they knew they could return again and again. Their daily prayer was:

Deliver me from the guilt of bloodshed, O God, the God of my salvation.
—Psalm 51:14

DELIVERANCE

J esus changed the world when He said to turn the other cheek to someone who slaps you. (See Matthew 5:39.) David grew up centuries before Jesus said this; his only understanding was that whatever you commit against someone, equal punishment can be returned to you. David pleaded with God, "Deliver me from the guilt of bloodshed, O God, the God of my salvation" (Psalm 51:14).

David wasn't asking for forgiveness here but was asking God to save him from equal punishment. He recognized how far he had fallen into sin and wanted to be rescued from the same consequences he caused others.

David had already borne the death of Bathsheba's first baby and rightful heir to his throne, due to his own affair and murder. He didn't want God to end his own life early because of his sinful behavior. He turned to God as his salvation rather than as a vengeful being. If only we would turn to God, pleading with Him as Someone who wants to save us rather than punish us, perhaps we would have a more intimate relationship with Him.

Because David could turn to God at the lowest point of his life, he wrote:

> *My tongue shall sing aloud of Your righteousness.*
> *–Psalm 51:14*

CAN YOU HEAR ME NOW?

Today's title was the advertising slogan for a popular cell phone network. In the commercials, the actor would ask someone on a cell phone, "Can you hear me now?" The response, although never spoken, came through loud and clear every time: Yes! I can hear you now—due to your network's superiority!

"My tongue shall sing aloud of Your righteousness" (Psalm 51:14). As the cell phone company wanted its commercial catchphrase ringing in our ears, so David wanted everyone to know about God's righteousness. He wasn't boasting about how he returned to God, nor about once being lost but now being found. He wasn't boasting about his relationship with God but about God's relationship with him.

David pointed out that God is true to His promise to help those of us who are lost in sin. He was exclaiming to God, "Because You heard me now—here at my lowest point—and You saved me, Your righteousness will be my slogan." David then asked God to:

Open my lips, and my mouth shall show forth Your praise.
–Psalm 51:15

PRAISE

Have you ever tried to praise God when things are going badly? Have you ever tried to tell God what you appreciate about His character when your own character is being tested in the fire?

I've been there. When I hated everything, when I was losing everything in my life, when I didn't have anything positive to say to God, a friend told me, "Time to praise God!" My friend then "forced" me to praise God every day no matter how I felt.

Praising God does not come naturally, especially when we are down and out. Yet here was David, a wretched sinner like you and me, telling God: "Open my lips, and my mouth shall show forth Your praise" (Psalm 51:15).

When you are hanging by the last thread of the end of your rope, ask God to help you say a praise. When you spew out a praise through gritted teeth about God's forgiving, loving, enduring, slow-to-anger … character, God can do something powerful in your life. David again showed us, and would for the rest of our psalm, that we need to relinquish control of self and let God lead—that God wants nothing other than *ourselves:*

> *You do not desire sacrifice, or else I would give it;*
> *You do not delight in burnt offering.*
> *–Psalm 51:16*

DAY 33

ALL I GOT

One sweltering summer day, I tried to climb Half Dome at Yosemite National Park. For those who haven't done this, the hike is extremely long, and the end—the actual climbing up Half Dome—is done while hanging onto ropes and climbing a nearly vertical rock wall. After starting out before daybreak, excited about seeing the world from the top of this famous landmark, after giving it all I had all day long—I was too tired to finish. When I arrived at the rock wall, all I could do was touch the ropes and sit down in exhaustion.

"You do not desire sacrifice, or else I would give it; You do not delight in burnt offering" (Psalm 51:16). There wasn't an animal sacrifice that David could offer that would please God at that point. He couldn't offer up anything to erase his sins. David acknowledged—even in his tradition and culture of Jewish sacrifices—that there must be something more, something greater, than a symbol of relationship with God.

Like David, who knew that he must offer himself to God, we must give God "all we got"—our desires, our attitude, ourselves:

The sacrifices of God are a broken spirit, a broken and a contrite heart.
–Psalm 51:17

I WANT IT ALL

I want it all. I want success. I want fortune. I want to be important. I want the American Dream. I want it all. I really do. And in this wanting it all, I have become just like Satan, that serpent of old, the devil himself. "The sacrifices of God are a broken spirit, a broken and a contrite heart" (Psalm 51:17).

David had it all, wanted more, slept with a married woman, covered his sin in intentional murder, and then penned these words. As did the devil, he wanted control over his life. He even wanted to play God by thinking every outcome of his decisions was under his control. Then David realized that God can't deal with our pride. God can help us only when we are broken.

A broken spirit and contrite heart are about being humble. We must come to God humbly, owning our mistakes and realizing that He can and will be with us if we sacrifice our egotistical, narcissistic, big-headed ways to Him. Let God work in your life. Let God be God. He is the Creator; He knows what He's doing. Let go and let God have control. When we give Him our brokenness and humility for His action in our lives, we can trust that:

> *These, O God, You will not despise.*
> *–Psalm 51:17*

COME TO ME

These, O God, You will not despise" (Psalm 51:17). Yesterday, we talked about coming to God humbly and in brokenness, with a broken spirit and a contrite, or repentant, heart. We learned that when we do this, He will not turn away.

In the New Testament, Jesus would invite those who are burdened and weary to come to Him, a repetition of David's discovery that we can come to God and not be turned away.

Our society is filled with rejection. There are job applications that never make it past our submissions, relationships that never make it past the first date, text messages that are never returned. We are used to being rejected, we are hardened against it, and many times we simply expect it. When we are rejected, we work hard arranging things so that next time, we will be sure to make it on our own—avoiding the need to ask for help, and avoiding the risk of more rejection.

We are so against rejection that even in times of need, we are hesitant to ask for help. But David got past this; having messed up and sinned, he asked that God:

> *Do good in Your good pleasure to Zion.*
> *—Psalm 51:18*

ZION

Zion—what a city! It was the city God blessed and chose to be His own city. "Do good in Your good pleasure to Zion" (Psalm 51:18). David was probably thinking of Jerusalem, the city that was to house the Savior of the world—and crucify Him just outside its walls. David's invitation for God to do good to Zion carries a double meaning.

First, Zion was his own life. David was saying, Do what You please, whatever is acceptable to You in my own life; I relinquish control of it to You.

Second, Zion is your life and mine. David was allowing God to do whatever He wants in the lives of His people.

God does not abandon us when we sin. We are not left to our own wiles or wills. The Mayor of the city still loves us—dearly. When I come to God and say, Do good in my messed-up life because I am still valuable to You, I am relinquishing control to Him. He can then do good in my un-goodness. With our permission, God can enter our lives and:

> *Build the walls of Jerusalem.*
> *—Psalm 51:18*

BUILD THE WALLS

In the ancient world of King David, walls served one purpose: to keep enemies out—to protect a city against invading forces.

"Build the walls of Jerusalem" (Psalm 51:18). With Zion representing humanity, as we talked about yesterday, here David asked for something from God—not forgiveness but protection. The enemy had attacked David with arrows of lust, shot from the bow of beautiful, unsuspecting Bathsheba. David's city walls crumbled, giving his attacker a stronghold in his life. To withstand future attacks, David asked to be surrounded and protected with God's walls.

When we try to keep sin out of our lives by guarding our city with our own walls, we fail. When Adam and Eve ate the forbidden fruit, they became like God, knowing good and evil—their own judges of what was right and what was wrong. When we judge for ourselves the morality of life, our "city" is not fortified by God's protective law. But when we accept God's protection for our lives:

Then You shall be pleased with the sacrifices of righteousness.
–Psalm 51:19

RIGHTEOUSNESS

O nce God builds walls of protection around us, life is a piece of cake, right? In fact, you will likely tell me that living a Christian life has many difficulties, and I would agree.

Walls must be built because the city dwellers know there is an enemy who wants to control or destroy them. Likewise, God builds walls around us because He knows, and we know, there is an enemy, Satan, who wants to control and destroy us.

"Then You shall be pleased with the sacrifices of righteousness" (Psalm 51:19). When we have God's protection in our lives, it doesn't mean the enemy will not attack, but rather that we will enjoy more freedom to obey God, leading to abundant and eternal life. Will we obey perfectly? Not if it's up to us. But when God is in our lives, we have the assurance of His protection. And when we do stumble and repent, our lives can still be a sacrifice to Him. He will take our iniquity—our guilt caused by sin—and transform it into triumphal stories of redemption.

When we see how God acts when the enemy attacks us, we can:

> *With burnt offering and whole burnt*
> *offering … offer bulls on Your altar.*
> *–Psalm 51:19*

THE CROSS

I have two children, a little girl and a little boy. When they were born, they were the cutest children you could ever imagine. And now, they are the most adorable kids you will meet. But here's the thing: When parents tell you how wonderful their children are, they are biased. Parents always think their child is more adorable than anyone else's.

Because we are Christians looking back into the Hebrew world of King David, perhaps we are biased. We may tie Christian understandings to the Hebrews. However, notice that David didn't refer to "the" altar but to "Your" altar. Was David claiming that God's altar was the foreshadowing of the Cross? The New Testament Christian church did build the Cross into its Jewish sacrificial system theology.

Forgiveness and protection from sin require the sacrifice of Jesus—God's Son on God's altar. Psalm 51 emphasizes that we must relinquish control of our own lives. God needs to re-create sinners. The Jewish sacrifices fall short of completing this re-creation; only Christ's sacrifice can accomplish a renewal of our lives. Jesus is the Forgiver, Jesus is the Savior, Jesus is the reason repentance is accessible.

DAY 40

MOVING FORWARD

We have taken a journey in this book—a sinner's journey. While Psalm 51 was written by and about King David, any one of us could replace his name with ours because we find ourselves in the same scenario: guilty and in need of God.

The entire Psalm was built around a pleading for God to recreate, to restore, and to renew a sinner's life. Our plea must always be our need of God. When we believe we are self-sufficient, when we believe we can handle life with our own morality, when we believe we can endure the temptations the enemy throws at us, we will fall. But praise be to God that when failure comes, the real scandal is that we can turn to Him who is quick to save, quick to re-create our lives, and quick to place a spirit of willing submission in our hearts. The scandalous love and sacrifice of God for our mistakes through His Son Jesus Christ makes us clean.

Pray with me:

Lord God, my life is Yours.
Lord God, my mistakes are Yours.
Lord God, my guilt is Yours.
Lord God, create me, restore me, renew me.
And use me as only Yours.
Amen.